America's
NATIONAL PARKS

AN INSIDER'S GUIDE TO UNFORGETTABLE PLACES AND EXPERIENCES

NATIONAL PARKS CONSERVATION ASSOCIATION

npca.org

TIME HOME ENTERTAINMENT

PUBLISHER Jim Childs

VICE PRESIDENT, BUSINESS DEVELOPMENT & STRATEGY Steven Sandonato

EXECUTIVE DIRECTOR, MARKETING SERVICES Carol Pittard

EXECUTIVE DIRECTOR, RETAIL & SPECIAL SALES Tom Mifsud

EXECUTIVE PUBLISHING DIRECTOR Joy Butts

EDITORIAL DIRECTOR Stephen Koepp

EDITORIAL OPERATIONS DIRECTOR Michael Q. Bullerdick

DIRECTOR, BOOKAZINE DEVELOPMENT & MARKETING Laura Adam

FINANCE DIRECTOR Glenn Buonocore

ASSOCIATE PUBLISHING DIRECTOR Megan Pearlman

ASSISTANT GENERAL COUNSEL Helen Wan

ASSISTANT DIRECTOR, SPECIAL SALES Ilene Schreider

SENIOR BOOK PRODUCTION MANAGER Susan Chodakiewicz

DESIGN & PREPRESS MANAGER Anne-Michelle Gallero

BRAND MANAGER Nina Fleishman

ASSOCIATE PREPRESS MANAGER Alex Voznesenskiy

SPECIAL THANKS TO Christine Austin, Jeremy Biloon, Rose Cirrincione, Lauren Hall Clark, Jacqueline Fitzgerald, Christine Font, Jenna Goldberg, Hillary Hirsch, Suzanne Janso, David Kahn, Mona Li, Amy Mangus, Robert Marasco, Kimberly Marshall, Amy Migliaccio, Nina Mistry, Dave Rozzelle, Adriana Tierno, Vanessa Wu

We welcome your comments and suggestions about Time Home Entertainment Books. Please write to us at:

Time Home Entertainment Books
Attention: Book Editors
P.O. Box 11016
Des Moines, IA 50336-1016

If you would like to order any of our hardcover Collector's Edition books, please call us at 1-800-327-6388, Monday through Friday, 7 a.m. to 8 p.m., or Saturday, 7 a.m. to 6 p.m., Central Time.

Design by www.reitdesign.com

Produced by Downtown Bookworks Inc.

Licensed by the National Parks Conservation Association

America's
NATIONAL PARKS

AN INSIDER'S GUIDE TO UNFORGETTABLE PLACES AND EXPERIENCES

NATIONAL PARKS CONSERVATION ASSOCIATION

npca.org

FEATURING THE PHOTOGRAPHY OF:

JUSTIN BAILIE
GEORGE H.H. HUEY
ROBERT GLENN KETCHUM
THOMAS D. MANGELSEN
DAVID MUENCH
MARC MUENCH
IAN SHIVE
MATTHEW TURLEY
ART WOLFE

Text Scott Kirkwood & Elizabeth Meyers
Photo Editing Scott Kirkwood & Nicole Yin

CONTENTS

When I envision a 100th birthday party, I picture a grandparent surrounded by children, grandchildren, and great-grandchildren—generations gathered around a birthday cake, bathed in the warm glow of candlelight, each one telling stories of favorite moments with the honoree. As the National Park Service prepares to celebrate its 100th birthday in 2016, a similar image comes to mind: generations of park lovers gathered around the warmth of a campfire, sharing tales of their adventures in some of America's favorite places.

The book you're holding in your hands attempts to capture some of those moments, some of the scenes that can be experienced by any American for a few gallons of gas and a humble entrance fee: hiking through the giants of the Redwoods, biking along the carriage roads of Acadia, standing before the Lincoln Memorial, or wandering the ruins of Mesa Verde. More adventurous souls may try ice climbing on a glacier in Wrangell-St. Elias, whitewater rafting in the Grand Canyon, or rock climbing in Yosemite. But you don't need to backpack in the Rockies or snorkel in the Florida Keys to experience our national parks in a life-changing way. You just need a map, a bottle of water, and a camera.

I've had a personal connection to these places since I was a child. I grew up kayaking in Mather Gorge, part of the C&O Canal National Historical Park in Maryland. After college, I paddled rivers in the Grand Canyon, Canyonlands, and Dinosaur National Monument. My wife and I attended the opening of the Martin Luther King, Jr. Memorial in Washington, D.C. I've climbed the Grand Teton with my two sons, and camped on Dry Tortugas with all three of my children. And I've taken my entire family to see my father's name carved in the granite wall of the Vietnam Memorial.

FOREWORD

Americans have been flocking to these special places ever since photographers and artists started documenting them at the end of the 19th century. When the Park Service was created in August 1916, three dozen park units existed, among them Acadia, Crater Lake, Glacier, Sequoia, and, of course, Yellowstone and Yosemite. The 100 years that followed saw the creation of a unified system that contains the best our nation has to offer—history, culture, wildlife, and scenic vistas—all brought to life by a park ranger with an iconic hat and a welcoming smile. The next hundred years are about expanding that audience and ensuring the parks' place in the hearts of all Americans.

If you stop at a scenic turnout at any well-known national park, you'll likely hear a handful of languages spoken by visitors from Europe and Asia and nearly every other continent. But you may not see many visitors from urban areas, from impoverished communities, or Americans from racially and ethnically diverse backgrounds. School groups, once fixtures in our parks, are missing out due to parks' staffing cutbacks. Campfire talks and ranger-led hikes are fewer and farther between. And as the federal government looks to make even more cuts to park budgets in this time of austerity, park superintendents will be faced with more difficult decisions. The only way to ensure that our parks remain a priority is to show our leaders that we still value these places.

My organization, the National Parks Conservation Association, has been around nearly as long as the National Park Service; we'll mark our 93rd birthday this fall. With the help of our 600,000 members and supporters, we work to ensure that every park remains as vital as it was the day that this nation decided it should be preserved for the ages. As our parks approach their centennial and enter their second hundred years, we all have a role to play. Take a child to your favorite park. Join a park's friends group. The next time a park is threatened, write your members of Congress or send a letter to the editor of your local paper. Buy this book. Go for a hike. Volunteer at a park in your own backyard. With 397 national park units sprinkled across our country, there's probably one closer than you think. And if you need a little inspiration, just turn the page.

TOM KIERNAN
President
National Parks Conservation Association
Washington, D.C.

⛰ THE MOUNTAINS

The view from a mountain trail is like no other view—not simply because of the perspective it provides, but because you've earned that perspective one step at a time, one breath at a time. Some mountains beg to be climbed, but all mountains beg to be photographed. The jagged peaks of Grand Teton, instantly identifiable in any photo. The granite faces of Yosemite, where the tiniest speck turns out to be a rock climber. Every corner of Glacier National Park, named for the chisels of ice that carved out the landscape, which are vanishing far too fast.

The most spectacular landscapes seem to draw the most spectacular species. Bison that stand like trees, and seem equally immovable—as if they have been there forever, unconcerned with the snow, the wind, the sun, or the rain. Wolves, reintroduced to Yellowstone in 1995, now thriving and returning the ecosystem to balance. Wolverines that are very rarely seen, and that traverse a mountain with the ease of a pedestrian crossing the street. Grizzlies, the kings of this jungle—powerful enough to bring down a moose or an elk, but willing to eat roots, seeds, and berries when it's all that's on offer.

Americans have always been drawn to the mountains, and nostalgia is now part of the attraction. We come for the things we expect to see: the old lodges, the classic yellow buses of Yellowstone, and the old red buses of Glacier. And we come for the surprises: a field of wildflowers, an empty cabin at 10,000 feet, an alpine lake, a coyote that wasn't expecting to see you either.

OPPOSITE: Tunnel View overlook in Yosemite National Park, California, is one of the most famous views in all of the 397 national park units. Since its construction in 1933, it has been thrilling visitors with striking vistas of iconic features such as the massive granite form of El Capitan, a favorite with experienced rock climbers, and the 620-foot sheer drop of Bridalveil Falls.

GLACIER

Glacier National Park in Montana has the mountain scenery and the diverse wildlife that visitors come to expect in a park experience, putting it consistently at the top of most "favorite park" lists. Lake McDonald Lodge and Many Glacier Hotel are among the most popular historic lodges in all the parks; the summer months always sell out, so plan ahead. Willing to rough it? The park's 13 campgrounds provide 1,000 sites to pitch your tent. **ABOVE:** A bighorn sheep seems to strike a pose while showing off a talent for climbing rocky terrain (1), and a marmot is framed by the lush grasses and wildflowers of an alpine meadow (4). A hiker pauses to enjoy the view of Lower Grinnell Lake (2), named for turn-of-the-century park advocate George Bird Grinnell, who happened to count Teddy Roosevelt among his friends. Restored Ford motor coaches (3) have been offering visitors since the 1930s (with some recent refurbishment) a great way to enjoy Going-to-the-Sun-Road—an engineering marvel that winds through the Rockies' peaks. The buses' canvas tops roll back so you won't miss any of the dramatic scenery. Be sure to make a tour reservation with Glacier Park Inc. to ride in one of these vintage buses and be regaled with park history by your knowledgeable driver.

1

2

4

3

The view of Grinnell Lake and the view along the Grinnell Glacier Trail **(1)**. A historic photo of Sun Point Chalet **(2)** illustrates why the park is often called the Switzerland of North America. Glacier provides the core of one of the largest remaining grizzly bear populations in the lower 48 states and one of the most intact ecosystems in North America **(3)**. When you go for a hike, be sure to make noise to help limit surprise encounters—which aren't all that uncommon given current estimates of 300 grizzlies that call the park home. Although snow-covered peaks abound **(4)**, the number of glaciers in the region has declined from 150 in 1850 to only 26 today. Visit the park soon to see them, because by 2020 they could all be gone due to a warming shift in the climate.

Bighorn sheep are among the most common species visitors will find in Glacier National Park, Montana.

Three mountain goats poised precariously on a cliff face. Viewed either up close or, just as often, as tiny white dots in the distance, these creatures are right at home on the rocky ground of the park.

GRAND TETON

A view of the Snake River with the sun setting over the Tetons in the background (the same shot Ansel Adams made famous in 1942), taken from a pull-out on the main park road **(1)**. A mountaineer in Grand Teton National Park **(2)**, one of the more popular destinations for the sport. A bison looks through sagebrush in Antelope Flats **(3)**, a great place to find wildlife such as pronghorn antelope, which live there during the summer.

Its neighbor to the north, Yellowstone, grabs most of the headlines, but Wyoming's Grand Teton National Park offers plenty of wildlife-watching opportunities as well. **ABOVE**: Two grizzlies in a field of wildflowers (1). Pronghorn (2) spend most of the year in the park, but development pressures have made their trek between summer habitats in Grand Teton and winter habitats 200 miles away even more perilous. A weary mountaineer takes a break (3). Horses on an open range (4) with the Tetons as a backdrop.

Sunset, Grand Teton National Park, Wyoming.

Wildflowers in the Mazama Ridge, Mount Rainier National Park, Washington. There's no way to pinpoint the arrival of wildflowers in advance, but given the range in elevations, there's a good chance something will be blooming from spring through summer. When you arrive at the park's entrance gate, ask the ranger for the latest wildflower sightings.

Detail of the summit crater as seen from the highest point on Mount Rainier, Washington state. If you're planning a visit, the historic Paradise Inn is the perfect place to stay. Built in 1916, the lodge is generally open mid-May through early October, and offers easy access to hiking trails and amazing views of the park's peaks and meadows.

YELLOWSTONE

Yellowstone is where the mountains meet the plains. The park possesses some of the best wildlife-watching opportunities and iconic thermal features like the famous geyser, Old Faithful. **ABOVE**: Five coyote pups watch the world from outside their den **(1)**. Bison graze in a field of gold—a common sight **(2)**. A bison's bulk—it's North America's largest land mammal—belies the animal's capacity for running at speeds that top 30 miles per hour.

There really isn't a bad time to head to Yellowstone, but a visit in late spring is sure to be filled with young wildlife and green vistas, like the winding stream above (1). Fog rising off a hot spring around barren trees (2) creates a magical winter scene in Lower Geyser Basin. Winter is a great time for snowshoeing and cross country skiing and much smaller crowds, but fewer park lodges are open, so you'll want to book a room well in advance.

A coyote stands in grass along a stream. Coyotes are common predators in Yellowstone, often seen traveling through wide, open valleys hunting small mammals. Like wolves, coyotes are also capable of killing larger prey, especially when they hunt as a group. At about 30 pounds, coyotes can generally be distinguished from their much larger relative, the gray wolf, which ranges from 75 to 125 pounds.

The Lower Falls of the Yellowstone, made famous by American painter Thomas Moran in 1872, at a time when artists were first generating interest in many of the Western landscapes unknown among Americans in the East. At 308 feet, the park's tallest waterfall can be viewed from Lookout Point, Artist Point, and several other locations.

An overhead view of the Grand Prismatic Spring, the park's largest hot spring, measuring approximately 370 feet in diameter and more than 121 feet deep. Yellowstone holds the planet's most diverse and intact collection of geysers, hot springs, mudpots, and fumaroles. All of these geothermal features are due to the fact that Yellowstone is actually a volcano—although it isn't expected to erupt for at least another thousand years.

YOSEMITE

Yosemite is known for landscapes more than wildlife, but those landscapes amaze—and there are dozens of ways to experience them. Hard-core athletes scale El Capitan, a mecca for "big wall" climbers. At nearly 5,000 feet above the Yosemite Valley floor, Half Dome (1) is a daunting sight, but each year thousands of people make the 16-mile round-trip journey in about 12 hours, climbing to the peak by holding on to metal cables the last 400 feet. Below, visitors preparing for a hike (2) and relaxing at the end (3). For a more leisurely hike, check out the half-mile trip to and from Bridalveil Falls, the 1-mile loop to Lower Yosemite Falls, or the 2-mile round-trip stroll to Mirror Lake. OPPOSITE: Yosemite Valley at night.

⌂ THE RED ROCKS

A s you hop in your rental car and launch your trip to the parks of Arizona, Utah, and New Mexico, the neon lights of Las Vegas may beckon in your rear-view mirror, tempting you to stay just one night. But the starlit skies of Arches, Grand Canyon, and Natural Bridges guarantee a much bigger payoff.

The first time you see the red-orange earth of Utah in the light of day, you might feel a little like Dorothy arriving in Oz. What once was black and white is suddenly bathed in Technicolor, making the granite cliffs of Yosemite seem just a little dull in comparison.

You may never really have cared much for geology. But right now, you're wondering how wind and water could shape limestone and sandstone into such magical forms. The park ranger's explanation of ice and erosion and prehistoric oceans makes perfect sense, but it's already slipping away from you, as you ride horseback through Bryce Canyon, its orange hoodoos like melting Creamsicles guiding the way. You wade in the chocolate-colored waters of Zion's Virgin River, splashing about like a kid on the first day of summer vacation. You cling to a metal chain bolted into the ground as you climb toward Angel's Landing. You stand beneath one of 2,000 arches in the park named for that very feature, and each one feels like a window to another world.

This is the Southwest. At times it feels like another planet—one that no one else has set foot on. You've got to try pretty hard to take a bad photograph here. But you won't see many as amazing as these....

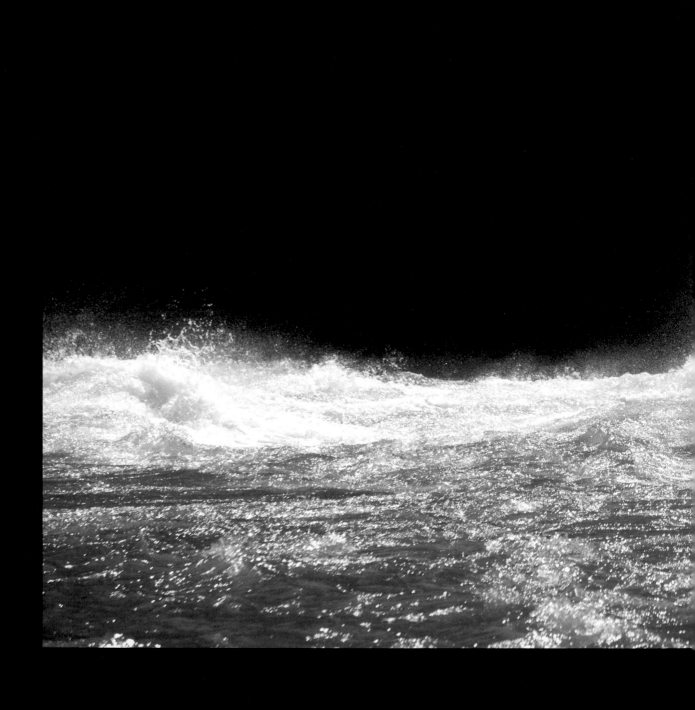

Rafting the Colorado River, Grand Canyon National Park, Arizona. Rafting trips can range from one day to a month, and provide the most genuine escape from cell phones and other modern intrusions. But you'll need to plan ahead: commercially guided trips often have wait-lists up to a year or two; if you want to bring your own boat, you'll need to enter a lottery. Learn more at www.nps.gov/grca.

Most people experience the Grand Canyon from the North Rim or the South Rim (OPPOSITE), but rafting the Colorado River provides the ultimate experience (1). A variety of river concessioners provide guided trips ranging in length from one day to 18 days. To run the river on your own, you'll need proven skills and one of the limited number of permits issued each year by the National Park Service. A group of people play volleyball in Redwall Cavern, a popular place to stop, eat lunch, and relax during a day on the river (2).

OPPOSITE: Courthouse Towers with the Organ and Tower of Babel formations, Arches National Park, Utah. A woman takes in the view at Partition Arch **(1)**. Geologic formations are a major attraction for visitors who marvel at the park's arches, spires, fins, and balanced rocks—many of which can be seen from viewpoints and short hikes accessible from the park's paved roads. The formation called Park Avenue **(2)** is a far cry from New York City.

Balanced Rock, Arches National Park, Utah, on a foggy winter morning. Like Park Avenue and Devil's Garden, Balanced Rock is one of the must-see destinations located just off the main park road.

Sunrise at the North Window, Arches National Park, Utah. The Windows section of the park is a quick and easy hike off the main park road, near Turret Arch and Double Arch.

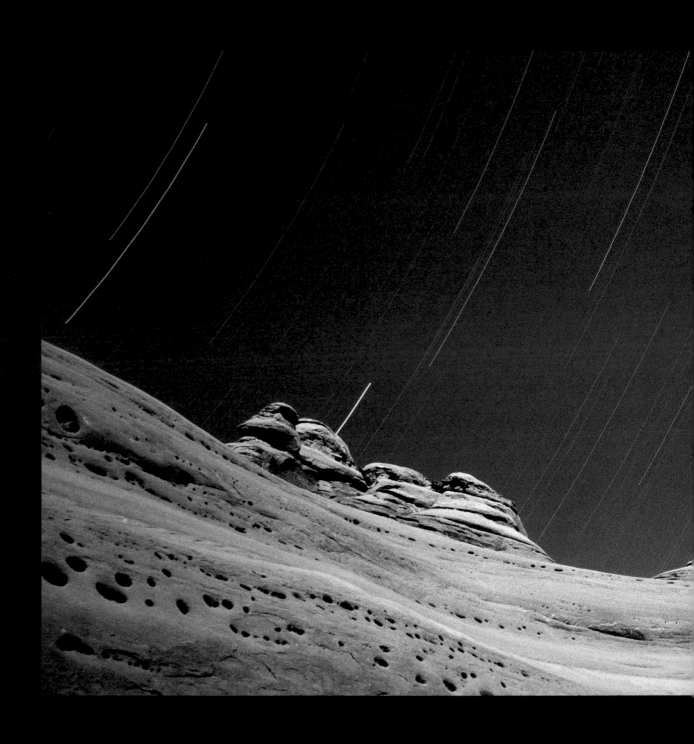

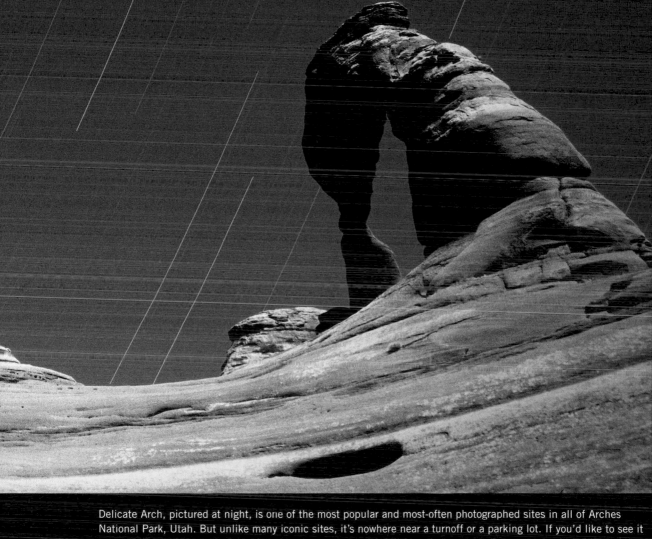

Delicate Arch, pictured at night, is one of the most popular and most-often photographed sites in all of Arches National Park, Utah. But unlike many iconic sites, it's nowhere near a turnoff or a parking lot. If you'd like to see it yourself, start at the Wolfe Ranch parking area and plan for a three-mile round-trip journey that will last two to three hours. Bring plenty of water, and if you head there at sunset, be sure to carry a flashlight for the return trip.

Sunrise from Sunset Point, Bryce Canyon National Park, Utah. A stunning view at any time of day, the gentle light of sunrise and sunset enhances the reds, oranges, and yellows created by minerals in the rock formations.

A lone hiker descends into Bryce Canyon's maze of rock formations, guided only by a dim flashlight.

Photographer Brad Beck was inside False Kiva in Canyonlands National Park, Utah, when a storm rolled in. After an hour of trying to capture a lightning strike, he was successful. Although the site is popular among photographers, the trail to False Kiva is unmarked and can only be reached via a three-hour hike.

The White Rim below Grandview Point, Canyonlands National Park, at sunset with the Abajo Mountains in the distance. Grandview Point Overlook is in the center of the park and easily accessible via the main road, but if you'd like to immerse yourself in the park experience, rent a four-wheel-drive vehicle and set aside two to three days to make the 100-mile journey along the rugged White Rim Road. You'll need a permit for any overnight stays in the backcountry, so contact the park in advance.

Adjusting a telescope for a stargazing party in Great Basin National Park, Nevada, one of the premier spots for night skies, thanks to the lack of development anywhere near the park. **OPPOSITE**: Natural Bridges National Monument, Utah, another site where stars sparkle in some of the country's darkest night skies. But you'll need daylight to see the park's natural sandstone bridges, which were cut over millennia by streams.

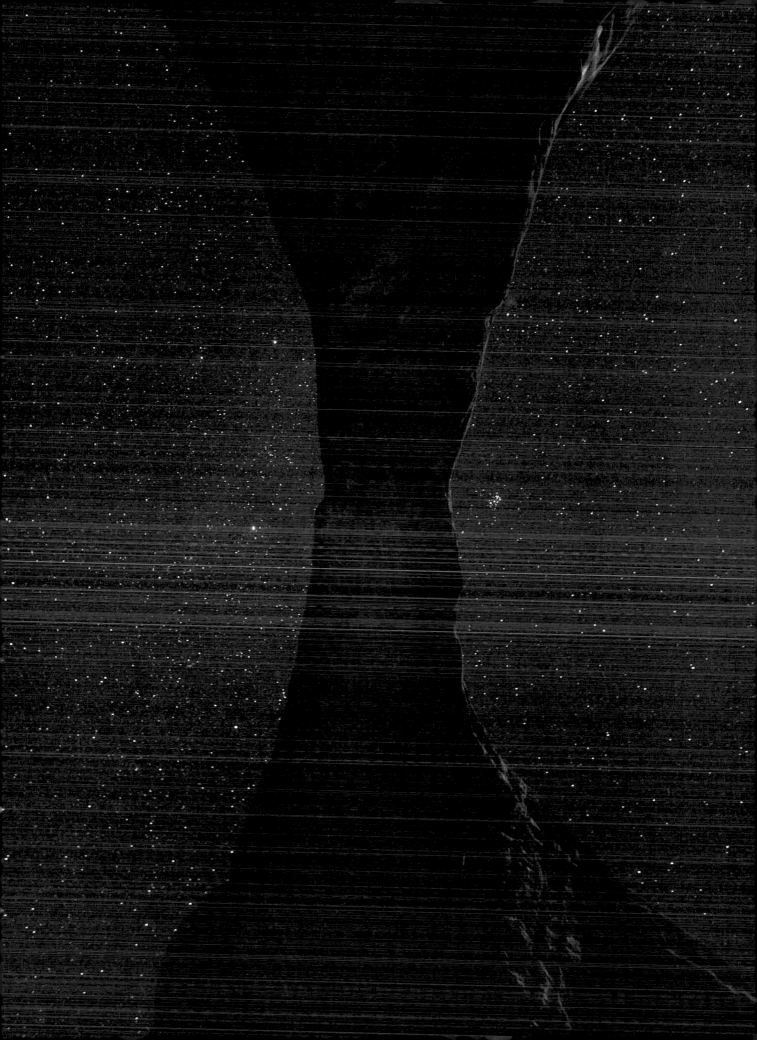

Park visitors stargazing in Great Basin National Park, Nevada, which features some of the clearest night skies in the country. You can join Great Basin's "Dark Rangers" for astronomy programs every Tuesday, Thursday, and Saturday night from Memorial Day to Labor Day; the park provides high-powered telescopes to bring the stars even closer (see previous spread). Check the park's website for more details: www.nps.gov/grba.

Petrified trees, which are roughly 215 million years old, litter the Arizona landscape. Most visitors to Petrified Forest National Park in Arizona drive through, spending about two to three hours lingering at viewpoints and walking on trails along the main park road. Each year 600,000 people visit the park, many attempting to time their arrival with wildflowers that tend to peak in May and July.

Zion is defined by the Virgin River, which flows through its canyons. Fall is an excellent time to see all the Utah park has to offer, including the Great White Throne, named by Methodist minister Frederick Vining Fisher in 1916.

The Watchman, which appears to watch over Zion Canyon's entrance (1); and the Temple of Sinawava (2)—part of the "Narrows," where visitors can splash through the riverbed for 16 miles, with the help of a walking stick or two.

Don't miss out on hiking the well-known Angel's Landing if you visit Zion National Park—unless you've got a paralyzing fear of heights, that is. Take the park's free shuttle to the Grotto shuttle stop and set aside about four hours for the five-mile, round-trip trek. The climb begins with a gradual ascent on a well-traveled trail, then rises nearly 1,500 feet above the Virgin River, through a series of switchbacks called Walters Wiggles—named after the park's first superintendent, who, back in 1925, paid workers $3.25 a day to carve out the winding path. Near the very end, you'll find a steep, narrow ridge with chains bolted into the earth, for hikers to grasp. Just remember: don't look down. OPPOSITE: The Crack, also known as the Chute, is just below one of Zion National Park's most famous slot canyons, called the Subway. Here, the Left Fork of North Creek is funneled through a narrow crack in red sandstone.

THE TREES

They are the biggest living things on earth and they are the oldest living things on earth. Many of the coastal redwoods and giant sequoias found in California's national parks are taller than the Statue of Liberty, and some have stood for 3,000 years. But the feeling you get when standing among them can't be measured in inches or feet, in days or in years. You are a child who snuck into the grown-ups' party. You are a character in a fairy tale. You crane your neck to see the treetops, but it's impossible. You imagine what it would be like to climb upon their limbs, and then you do—walking along a downed tree, your arms outstretched. You wonder what it would have been be like to see it fall. You wonder just how long ago it happened. And you wonder how long it will remain laying here, the biggest bench you've ever seen.

At the top of a mountain or the edge of a canyon, you can't resist the urge to yell, to see where your voice will go. In any deep forest, you feel obligated to whisper, as if you are in a place of worship. It's spring in the heart of Olympic's Hoh rainforest, and moss clings to every surface as if hiding a secret. It's summer in the Grand Tetons, and wind whispers through aspens, the sound of water rushing through a stream. It's a crisp fall day in Shenandoah, and a carpet of maple leaves crunches beneath your feet, announcing your every move. It's winter in the Rockies, and a blanket of pine needles cushions each step, the earth springing back beneath your feet like a trampoline.

You pull your camera from your pocket and take a photo, but it is impossible to capture a forest in two dimensions. Well, almost impossible.

OPPOSITE: A hiker takes in the splendor of Redwood National Park, California.

Slash Pines, Pinelands, Everglades National Park, Florida.

Grove of aspens, Grand Teton National Park, Wyoming.

Bristlecone pine, Mount Washington, in Great Basin, Nevada. Bristlecone pines are the longest-living trees on earth—some survive as long as 5,000 years. Ask a park ranger for directions to one of the several groves of trees: Wheeler Peak Grove, the most accessible grove in the park, is located on the northeast side of Wheeler Peak, reached by a one and a half-mile trail from Wheeler Peak Campground; Mount Washington (ABOVE) contains the largest grove of bristlecone pines in the park, but the lack of developed trails makes it difficult to access.

GREAT SMOKY MOUNTAINS

It's no secret that fall is the time to head to Great Smoky Mountains National Park, Tennessee, where you'll find a mosaic of red maple, sugar maple, white oak, and tulip poplar trees **(1, 2)**. **OPPOSITE:** An autumn cascade in Little River Canyon.

The ponds, streams, lakes, and mossy temperate rainforests of Olympic National Park in Washington are perfect for amphibians like this red-legged frog.

Black-tailed deer (1) are common throughout the park. A barred owl (3) is among the 300 or so different kinds of birds found there. The Hoh Rainforest provides more shades of green than the local paint shop (2). Although Olympic contains the Pacific Northwest's largest block of temperate rainforest and old-growth forest, it also captivates with glacier-capped mountains and rugged coastline.

REDWOODS

OPPOSITE: Redwood National Park is home to the world's tallest trees, reaching 200 to 300 feet or more in height; the extra moisture provided by ocean fog helps them grow so tall. **ABOVE**: A newt clings to a twig, providing a surprising splash of color **(2)**. Getting out on foot is the best way to see the park **(1 AND 3)**, and with more than 200 miles of trails, there's plenty of ground to cover. Bicycles are also welcome on all the park's paved roads and on a number of backcountry trails, including some old logging roads that have been rehabilitated.

Detail of aspen leaves, Rocky Mountain National Park, Colorado.

OPPOSITE: Parker Group, Sequoia National Park, California. Established in 1890 to protect the area's giant sequoias, this is the country's second national park. Some of its trees are estimated to be between 1,800 and 2,700 years old. ABOVE: A visitor to Sequoia National Park, 1910.

1

2

OPPOSITE: Virginia's Shenandoah National Park is just over an hour from Washington, D.C., but a world away. The park contains more than 500 miles of hiking trails, including 101 miles of the Appalachian Trail, but its most famous feature is Skyline Drive, a scenic byway that runs 105 miles north and south along the crest of the Blue Ridge Mountains. If you're planning to visit in the fall, aim for the middle of the week, as the route is packed with cars most fall weekends. Bypass the traffic by bicycling Skyline Drive, but be sure to take care on blind curves and be ready to earn your energy bar on the road's steep hills. ABOVE: A metallic jumping spider (1), and the hardwood forest of Shenandoah (2).

Tents in Curry Village, Yosemite Valley, California. More than 300 tents of various sizes stand among the trees, offering visitors rather rustic shelter, including fold-out cots, a heater, and a light or two. In the winter, guests can walk to the ice-skating rink and the rest of the village's accommodations. To learn more visit www.yosemitepark.com.

Jeffrey pine, on Sentinel Dome, one of the more popular hikes affording views of Yosemite Valley. Start at the Sentinel Dome and Taft Point trailhead, six miles east of the Bridalveil Creek Campground turnoff. Enjoy a moderate hike of 2.2 miles round trip through forest and wildflower-filled meadows, which generally peak in July.

The middle doesn't get much respect: "middle of the road," "middle of the pack," the "middle of nowhere." But the middle of the country holds gems often overlooked by those who jet to the mountains or head to the coast to get away from it all.

The Great Smoky Mountains—the very definition of a forest, and one of the nation's most visited parks. The Great Lakes parks, defined by water—Apostle Islands, Isle Royal, Pictured Rocks, and Voyageurs. Mammoth Cave—the longest cave in the world, with more than 360 miles of mapped passages. Tallgrass Prairie National Preserve, which protects a simple landscape that once covered the Midwest but has largely been erased by agriculture.

Take a road trip to these diverse park units and you'll find yourself in the middle of it all.

OPPOSITE: The Blue Ridge Parkway runs north and south 469 miles, and connects Shenandoah National Park in Virginia with Great Smoky Mountains National Park in North Carolina. Though perhaps outside the stereotype of a typical national park, the parkway's scenic overlooks and picnic areas make it the most visited park unit in the country.

The distinctive landscape of Badlands National Park in South Dakota reveals layers of sediment such as sand, silt, and clay that have been deposited over the course of millions of years. Cedar Pass Lodge houses the only lodging, gift store, and restaurant in the park. Cabins are booked early, so plan ahead. Two designated campgrounds are also available: Cedar Pass Campground, which has 96 sites with scenic views of the Badlands formations, and Sage Creek Primitive Campground, which is free of charge, but offers no running water. Visitors can also stay at the Badlands Inn, located just outside the park.

If you visit the Badlands' popular North Unit in the summer, head to the Ben Reifel Visitor Center for ranger-led tours, including fossil walks, prairie walks, and geology talks, all offered daily, and night-sky programs Friday through Monday evenings.

View of the Rio Grande from the cliffs along the hot springs trail to Rio Grande Village. The river separates Mexico (on the right) from the United States (left). Big Bend National Park is sometimes referred to as "three parks in one" because its 800,000 acres include mountain, desert, and river environments. Fall and spring are usually warm and pleasant. Summers are hot, although temperatures vary greatly between the desert floor and the Chisos Mountains

River tours of the Rio Grande are among the more popular activities in this park, which runs along the border of Texas and Mexico. Contact Big Bend River Tours, located three miles from the western entrance to Big Bend National Park.

A kayaker dropping off of The Spout on a stormy day at Great Falls of the Potomac, which separates Maryland and Virginia, just northwest of Washington D.C.. On the Maryland side, the C&O Canal National Historical Park is your starting point, and in Virginia, park headquarters are along the George Washington Memorial Parkway. If you're planning a visit to D.C. and sticking to public transportation, you can rent a bike in Georgetown and pedal the 13 miles to Great Falls along the C&O towpath for a great day trip.

Most of Americans' favorite places are near water, and the Great Lakes parks obviously have it in spades. **OPPOSITE:** a kayaker at Huginnin Cove, Isle Royale National Park, Michigan. The park is an island accessible only by boat or seaplane, and is a great place for backcountry camping. Don't forget your fishing pole if you want to catch your own dinner from Lake Superior or one of the island's inland lakes. Fall scenery from Voyageurs National Park **(1)**, Minnesota. Wild berries **(2)** collected on an early summer day, Isle Royale National Park. A misty sunrise at Chippewa Harbor **(3)**, Isle Royale National Park.

Each year more than six million people head to Great Smoky Mountains National Park to hike its 800 miles of trails, and to see the historic log cabins, cantilevered barns, and charming old churches of Cades Cove. Many drive the seven-mile road to take in 360-degree views from the observation tower on Clingmans Dome. They also come to see one or two of the park's 1,500 black bears, and if they're lucky, they just may see an elk, reintroduced to the park in 2001. **ABOVE**: Oconaluftee River in spring flow.

Kentucky's parks offer hidden gems that are deep underground or deep in the forest. If you head to Mammoth Cave **(1)**, sign up for the Snowball Tour, which leads visitors into a gypsum-encrusted chamber. The Focus on Frozen Niagara tour, offered in summer, gives amateur shutterbugs a chance to practice cave photography without the fear of tourists tripping over their tripods. Highlights at Cumberland Gap National Historic Park include a tour of the Hensley Settlement, a 20th-century homestead atop Brush Mountain, where trails lead to lush stands of birch, hickory, oak, and maple trees **(2)**. If you spend the night in the area, skip the chain hotels, head to quaint Cumberland Manor, and ask the owners where you can find some authentic Bluegrass music **(3)**.

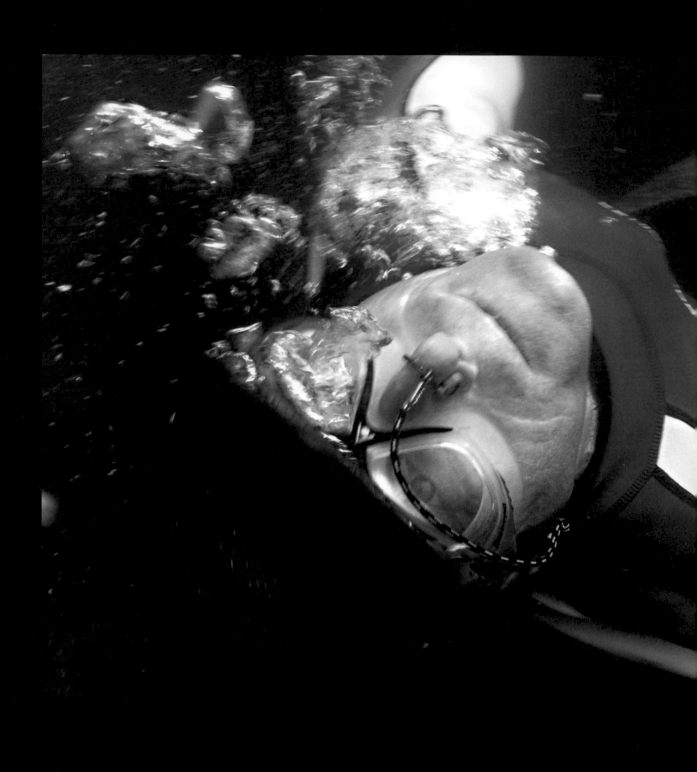

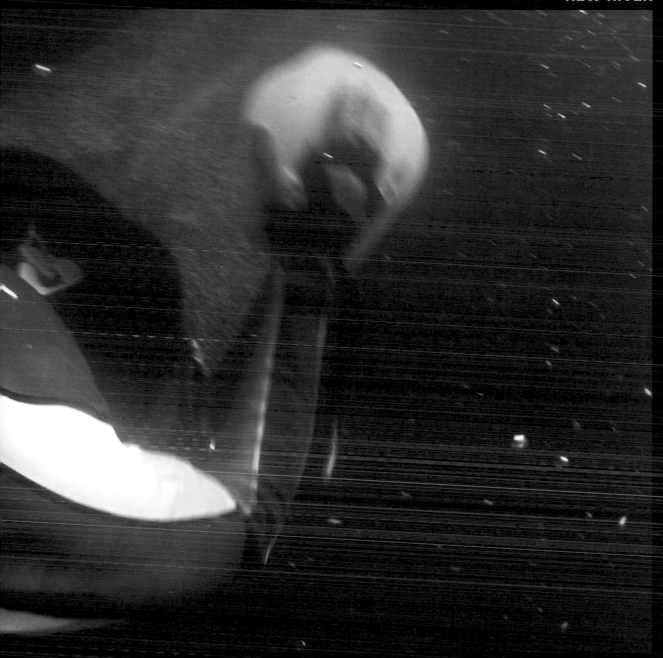

Most people who visit New River Gorge, West Virginia, do their best to stay above the water, hiring whitewater rafting guides from North American River Runners, ACE Rafting, or Wildwater Unlimited in nearby Minden, West Virginia. Here though, local Steve O'Keefe demonstrates a sport called squirtboating. Like kayaks with a flatter top, squirtboats allow athletes to go under the water, maneuvering with huge paddles that fit on their hands like gloves. Each sequence of calculated spins and turns through the river bottom can last as long as 40 seconds.

ABOVE: New River Gorge offers hiking and whitewater rafting. Every October, on Bridge Day, people can BASE jump or rappel from the top of the New River Gorge Bridge, 876 feet above the river below. Not quite so bold? Just walk across the bridge and enjoy music and the chili cook-off in downtown Fayetteville.

Tallgrass Prairie protects a sliver of prairieland (3) that once characterized 170 million acres of North America. Spring and summer are the ideal times to visit—from the last Saturday in April through the last Sunday in October, prairie bus tours led by knowledgeable rangers run every day at 11 a.m. Step off the bus to run your hands through the big bluestem grass and ask rangers like Jeff Rundell (2) about box turtles (4) and northern leopard frogs (1) that call the region home.

Tallgrass Prairie National Preserve, in Kansas, has a fledgling buffalo herd that was established by bringing 13 bison from Wind Cave National Park in South Dakota, in October 2009. Three calves had been born as of winter 2012, returning a keystone species to the landscape.

⚘ THE DESERT

With words like "death" and "devil," "dry" and "last chance" scattered all over the map, the desert parks may seem entirely inhospitable to newcomers. The desert's permanent residents rarely come out during the day, and they are very rarely cute or cuddly or the least bit furry. Its plants are prickly, and seem ready to lash out at anyone who dares to get too close.

The desert is a land of extremes, and many of its visitors are drawn to those extremes, too. The rock walls of Joshua Tree are beloved by athletes in search of world-class climbing routes. The pavement-melting heat of Death Valley punishes ultra-marathoners who gather each year to test themselves by running 135 miles in 100-degree temperatures.

But the desert also holds rewards for those with just a few gallons of water, a hat, and a bottle of sunscreen. Death Valley's Racetrack Playa, where rocks seem to move of their own accord. The Dr. Suessian shapes of Joshua trees and organ pipe cactus, each more bizarre than the next. A miniature forest of teddy bear chollas that are so adorable you'll be tempted to touch them before you think better of it.

And none of it is without purpose. This is evolution's playground. The skin of a saguaro mimics an accordion, expanding to fill with water during a deluge in case months pass between raindrops. Kangaroo rats in Great Sand Dunes National Park can go their entire lives without drinking by metabolizing the water in seeds. When Mojave's desert tortoises sense an approaching storm, they dig holes to catch the water so they can drink from the puddles for days or even weeks.

The desert is no place for the weak or the unprepared. There are harsh lessons to be learned here, in a land where shelter and water are difficult to find. There is a reason so many religious prophets and mythical figures find wisdom in the desert: rewards await those who know where to look.

OPPOSITE: A lone sagebrush on a cracked desert plain looking toward Death Valley's Eureka Dunes, at more than 680 feet, California's tallest sand dunes. A sandstorm erupts in the distance, catching the dramatic light of sunset.

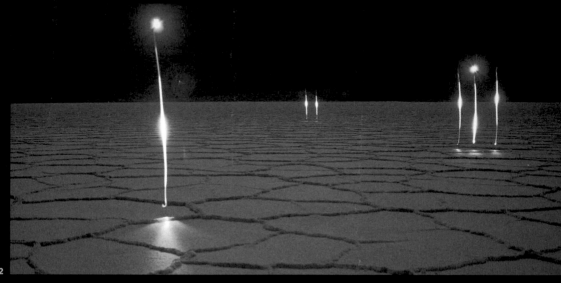

The name Death Valley scares off a lot of would-be visitors, but there is life in the California desert, like this coyote (1). A magical landscape (2) unfolds with the help of a few flashlights and a clever photographer (see page 120–121 for more). OPPOSITE: One of the "moving stones" that somehow cross the Racetrack Playa when no one is looking and leave their mark. Some believe a unique combination of rain and wind causes the movement, but the process has never been seen or captured on video. Death Valley is most welcoming in the fall, and in the spring, when heavy rains sometime lead to surprising explosions of wildflowers. It's a huge park with a lot to offer, so schedule at least four or five days to see it all.

A photographer at Zabriskie Point, one of Death Valley's most stunning views, not far from Furnace Creek. Come at sunrise or sunset, and don't forget your camera.

The splendor of Death Valley National Park in California doesn't fade when the sun goes down. With some of the darkest night skies in the National Park System, it's a stargazer's paradise, just two hours away from the bright lights of Las Vegas.

German photographers Cenci Goepel and Jens Warnecke capture the magic of the desert with a unique approach: one of them dons black clothing and wanders through the scene while moving a flashlight in various patterns, while the other leaves the camera's shutter open for five minutes or more to capture the surreal image. **OPPOSITE**: Organ Pipe Cactus National Monument, Arizona. **ABOVE**: Death Valley.

JOSHUA TREE

1

2

3

Rock climbers (1, 2) in Joshua Tree National Park, California; 8,000 routes for climbers of all skill levels make it a world-class destination for athletes. (BELOW) a young man takes in the scenery (3).

Joshua Tree silhouettes at sunrise. Joshua Tree is just two hours from Los Angeles and a popular spot for hiking, horseback riding, birding, and stargazing. Legend has it that Mormon pioneers named the tree after the Biblical figure, Joshua, seeing the limbs of the tree stretched toward the heavens, guiding the travelers westward.

If you've never thought of the desert as colorful, this shot of a summer thunderstorm over the Ajo Mountains, in Arizona, is sure to change your mind. If you want to see this part of Organ Pipe Cactus National Monument in person, reserve a spot on the park's free Ajo Mountain van tour. A ranger will show you the sights and explain the difference between an organ pipe cactus and a saguaro cactus on this three-hour tour.

OPPOSITE: Saguaro cacti, teddy bear cholla, and brittlebush, Saguaro National Park, Arizona. Saguaros grow about one inch per year the first eight years of their existence, and branches don't generally appear until the plant reaches 50 to 70 years of age; an adult saguaro can weigh as much as 12,000 pounds. **ABOVE**: Saguaros are shaped like accordions; their pleats can expand to take in enormous amounts of water, allowing the plant to endure long droughts.

National Parks Magazine associate editor Amy Marquis writes in a journal at White Sands National Monument, New Mexico, before enjoying a night under the stars. The park has ten primitive campsites, a short hike from the park's main road and available on a first come-first served basis.

The pure gypsum deposits that comprise the dunes of White Sands National Monument take on shades of blue at twilight. Experience their otherworldly appearance by car on the 16-mile Dunes Drive loop or up close on the Dune Life Nature Trail (one-mile loop).

THE LAST FRONTIER

With ice, cliffs, tundra, and wildlife at every turn, Alaska is one of the last untamed places in the world. History and nature exist side by side here. Hike on a glacier in Wrangell-St. Elias, then walk through an old copper mine that gave birth to the small town of McCarthy, where you'll spend the night. Or head to the southeast, and wander around Klondike Gold Rush National Historical Park in the morning, then spend the afternoon at Glacier Bay National Park watching icebergs calve into the water as kayakers glide past.

On the coast of Katmai National Park, you'll watch grizzlies lumber by, a few feet away, too busy foraging for food to even notice you. You can watch grizzlies fish for salmon at nearby Brooks Falls or head to Lake Clark and cast your own line in some of the best salmon habitat on the globe. Hop in the green bus and take a trip down Denali's Park Road, and it's unlikely you'll return without seeing a few grizzlies, caribou, or Dall sheep.

Unlike Yellowstone or Yosemite, there are no paved paths in Alaska's parks, no loops with visitor centers every few miles. This is a land where a three-hour drive is considered a short trip, where float planes and kayaks are as common as bicycles and taxicabs in Manhattan. Alaska is immense. You can't possibly see it all in one trip. So as soon as you end one visit, you just might start planning the next.

OPPOSITE: Gates of the Arctic National Park and Preserve is north of the Arctic Circle and far from any roads. Most visitors access the park by bush plane, starting from local villages.

OPPOSITE: Detail of fall colors in the Alaska tundra, Denali National Park. Leaves generally begin to change in August, with peak color usually the first or second week of September. A grizzly bear leads her cubs as they feast on ripening blueberries on Thorofare Pass in Denali **(1)**. Caribou **(2)**, moose **(3)**, and a wolf **(4)** are some of the wildlife visitors may encounter during a summer trip to the park. There's only one main road through Denali, and few private vehicles are allowed to drive it, so if you want to experience wildlife like this, you'll need to make reservations with one of several tour-bus operators just outside the park. Booking in advance is recommended. The park also offers shuttle buses if you want the freedom of hopping on and off at your leisure to take advantage of day hikes or photo opportunities.

DENALI

1

3

A bush plane lands on Kahiltna Glacier (1) at the 7,200-foot base camp of Mt. McKinley, North America's tallest peak. Each year, about 1,000 climbers attempt the ascent of the 20,000-foot mountain, and a little more than half are generally successful. An aerial image of a braided river (2). A bull moose keeps a watchful eye on his harem (3), with dwarf birch foliage in the background and the Alaska Range beyond.

Want to experience Denali's mountains up close and personal, while testing your physical endurance? A half-dozen mountaineering guide services are authorized to escort hardcore enthusiasts into some of the park's most stunning mountain landscapes.

Your best bet for experiencing the enchanting colors and shapes of the northern lights—or Aurora borealis—is (you guessed it!) to head north. In the winter months Alaska's national parks provide excellent opportunities to view this natural phenomenon. In this photograph, the northern lights illuminate the sky above the Toklat River in Denali National Park.

OPPOSITE: A park visitor explores a glacial ice cave, Glacier Bay National Park. **ABOVE:** Harbor seal on an iceberg, near Johns Hopkins Glacier. In 1992, 6,370 seals were counted in a park census, but their numbers dipped as low as 2,600 in recent years, a fact that is leading scientists to conduct intensive studies in the park.

For a unique perspective on the stunning natural scenery of Glacier Bay National Park and Preserve, consider booking a rafting trip with one of the many outfitters authorized to operate within the park. Private trips are also allowed with a permit from the National Park Service.

Close-up of a brown bear (1), taken from an elevated walkway near Brooks Lodge, where visitors can safely view the enormous animals from a few feet away. Look closely and you'll see bits of salmon on the bear's snout. This area's lakes and tributaries are critical to its bears, which rely on salmon to get their last layer of fat before hibernation. A grizzly bear cub walks through tall grass by Brooks River (2).

A woman holds Boletus mushrooms she picked in Chitina, just outside Wrangell-St. Elias National Park and Preserve, Alaska **(1)**. Surprisingly colorful stones found on the shore **(2)**. The small peaks flanking the Chokosna River valley reflected in one of the many small lakes encountered on the drive between Chitina and McCarthy, one of only two roads into the park. If you take the 60-mile McCarthy Road into the heart of the park, plan adequate time (it takes about three hours each way) and don't forget a spare tire and jack, in case you hit one of the spikes still found along parts of this former railway.

Photographer Paul Hassell captured this image on a 28-day expedition to Mt. Sanford's 16,300-foot summit as his group climbed up Sheep Glacier. The Wrangells, often called the Himalayas of North America, offer 20,000 square miles of secluded Alaskan wilderness—six times the size of Yellowstone. To appreciate some of the park's peaks without strapping on a pair of crampons, take the unpaved Nabesna Road from the Slana Ranger Station on a journey more than 40 miles into the park.

OPPOSITE: A stream meanders across tundra streaked with caribou trails. A man wades in a river in Lake Clark National Park, Alaska, to fly fish **(1)**. Visit from May through October if you want to try your hand fishing in some of the National Park System's most pristine waters. A native girl prepares smoked salmon **(2)**. The fish is a cornerstone of Alaskan native culture and the regional ecosystem. Nearby Bristol Bay is the world's largest sockeye salmon fishery, but the Bay and the national park are both threatened by a proposal to create the world's biggest open-pit copper and gold mine only 15 miles from the park's southern entrance. Conservation advocates are fighting hard to prevent the mine from destroying salmon habitat and bringing an end to native traditions.

THE COAST

The United States contains more than 12,000 miles of coastland, but those stretches designated as national parks are in a category all their own. If you're simply looking to enjoy some sun, surf, and sand with a cocktail at your side, look elsewhere, because these sights all beg to be actively explored.

The sea stacks of Olympic National Park, miniature mountains looming in the surf that somehow have endured eons of salt water crashing at their base. The wildlife of Channel Islands National Park, where sea lions frolic underwater and the endangered island fox wanders among the cliffs. The roiling and boiling waters of Hawaii Volcanoes National Park, where molten lava reaches into the sea and turns it into land one inch at a time. The rocky coast of Acadia, where you're better off leaving the sandals at home and bringing your hiking boots. The thousands of birds that call Everglades home and the manatees quietly lurking beneath your canoe, swimming through the River of Grass.

Beyond the smell of saltwater that fills the air, each of these places is as unique as every grain of sand underfoot.

OPPOSITE: A scuba diver swims beneath an underwater arch in Channel Islands National Park, California.

OPPOSITE: The Bass Harbor Head Lighthouse at sunset, Mt. Desert Island, Acadia National Park, Maine. Built in 1858, the lighthouse is still an active navigational aid, and the commander of the local Coast Guard unit lives on site in the keeper's house. It's a favorite subject for photographers, so don't forget to snap a few shots if you visit. Storm surf at sunrise along the Ocean Path, Mt. Desert Island **(1)**, and the charming town of Bar Harbor, where most park visitors spend a few nights **(2)**.

OPPOSITE: A kayaker exploring the Porcupine Islands. **ABOVE**: A young couple sitting on a lone rock in a calm, smooth lake on a foggy afternoon, Isle au Haut. Most of the land that now makes up Acadia was once owned by the Rockefeller family, and the carriage roads they constructed from 1913 to 1940 provide 45 miles of some of the best hiking, biking, and horseback riding in the region. Leave your car in the quaint town of Bar Harbor and jump back on and off the bus whenever you like. If you want to avoid the crowds, pack a picnic for your stroll along the 1.2-mile Ship Harbor Trail or head out for spectacular views of Somes Sound from the 2.5-mile Acadia Mountain Trail—both are loops.

Afternoon thunderstorms are common during the summer in south Florida, so bring a raincoat when you visit Biscayne National Park. You'll want to stay dry as you marvel at the dramatic cloudscapes that unfold before your eyes.

The roots of the red mangrove in Rubicon Keys extend into the water, making a mazelike refuge for young fish and other marine life.

The island fox, on Santa Cruz Island, Channel Islands, California—a critically endangered species whose numbers had dropped below 100 as recently as 2004 but have rebounded to as many as 1,200 thanks to restoration efforts that included captive breeding (1). A western gull with newborn chicks (2) on Anacapa Island, which is home to more than 15,000 of the birds.

Detail of succulents, or live-forevers, on Santa Cruz Island (1). These hardy plants store water in their leaves. There's plenty to see in the waters around the Channel Islands (2), and there's no shortage of dive shops on the mainland ready to outfit you with a wetsuit and flippers and take you to the best locations for snorkeling and diving.

Graceful, acrobatic, playful, social—the list of adjectives that can be used to describe California sea lions goes on and on. These engaging marine mammals are an entertaining sight for visitors to California's Channel Islands.

The Pacific chorus frog *(Pseudacris regilla)* is one of only two amphibian species found in Channel Islands National Park; the other is a salamander. It's possible you've heard recordings of this common frog species in the background of Hollywood films during nighttime scenes.

Northern fur seals and California sea lions share the beach at Point Bennett in summer. If you make the trip to San Miguel Island, be sure to set up a ranger-led hike to the point so you can be one of just a few hundred people who see this popular pinniped breeding beach each year.

A man enjoys the view looking over Potato Harbor at sunset on Santa Cruz Island.

A thunderhead photographed during sunset in Everglades National Park, captured by Florida photographer Brian Call, who enjoys visiting the park in August and September when the River of Grass is lush and green and ominous thunderstorms make for dramatic skies. The only drawbacks? The incredible heat and humidity—and those pesky mosquitoes.

Black skimmers photographed from a kayak in Everglades National Park (1). Birdwatchers prefer November through March and suggest bringing your binoculars to the Snake Bight area to see large flocks of roseate spoonbills, white pelicans, ibis, and even an occasional wild flamingo. Alligators, like this juvenile (3), can be found throughout the park, lurking in the water or sunning themselves just off a well-traveled path. The lighthouse on Loggerhead Key, Dry Tortugas National Park, located at the tip of the Florida Keys (2).

Paurotis Pond is usually active with wood storks, roseate spoonbills, great egrets (ABOVE), and ibis, through August. The pond closes to the public from January to about May to give endangered wood storks an undisturbed place to mate, but the nearby parking lot remains open and is a great place to watch their nesting activities.

A green sea turtle climbs ashore at Pu'uhonua o Honaunau National Historical Park, a sanctuary where ancient temples and ki'i (wooden carvings) whisper stories of the people who came before.

A local artisan crafts hats out of palm in Punalu'u (1), and a visitor enjoys locally grown lime and papaya just outside of Hawai'i Volcanoes National Park (2).

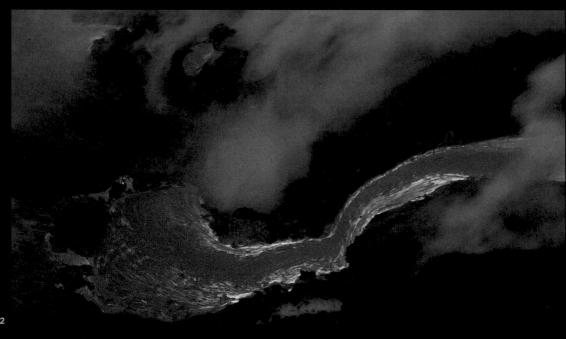

People watching lava flow into ocean **(1, 2, OPPOSITE)**, Kilauea Volcano, Hawai'i Volcanoes National Park, Island of Hawai'i. The process can be a beautiful one, but it is also quite dangerous: Visitors must hike miles to get to the water's edge, walking across sharp, jagged black lava, often in darkness. Like many park experiences, this one requires a bit of luck, because this brand of fireworks doesn't follow any particular schedule.

A castle or a ghost ship? Sea stacks off the coast of Olympic National Park, in Washington state, cast unusual shapes against the sky just after sunset. This view at Ruby Beach is easily accessible from Highway 101. Cruise just a bit farther south to camp overnight at Kalaloch Campground or experience the charm of a rustic—but well-appointed—cabin at Kalaloch Lodge.

The sprawling natural parks garner most of the headlines, but of the 397 park units in the nation, most are smaller sites devoted to America's history.

Mesa Verde and Chaco Culture tell the stories of native people who inhabited this country long before it was a country—long before there were any countries at all. They carved villages out of mountains, built structures oriented toward the heavens, and left many mysteries behind.

San Antonio's Missions illustrate the impact of Europe's colonial power in the 1700s, and the beautiful structures still host religious services 300 years after they were built. In St. Louis, an arch stretches across the skyline, marking the city where pioneers began their journey West. In New York, Ellis Island and the Statue of Liberty serve as monuments to the immigrants who boarded a boat armed with little more than the clothes on their backs and a few words of English.

And then there are the memorials to war. Empty fields that a park ranger brings to life with stories of young men far from home, fighting on someone's farm, fighting for the high ground, perhaps, or for a supply line, but ultimately, fighting for their ideals.

These sites tell the stories of individual men and women—our presidents, our writers, our poets, and our leaders in innovation, industry, politics, and civil rights.

These monuments celebrate our triumphs and remind us of our mistakes. They tell the stories of slavery, racism, and blood spilled in conflict, but they also tell the stories of our nation's first people, of a country that opened its doors to those in search of a better life, and of a man who rose above race to make a dream a reality.

OPPOSITE: Pueblo del Arroyo, Anasazi culture "great house," within Chaco Culture National Historical Park, New Mexico. Built between 900 and 1,000 years ago, and now easily accessible from the park's Canyon Loop Drive, much of this site, incredibly, has endured through time.

MESA VERDE

Mesa Verde, Spanish for "green table," focuses on the history and culture of the Ancestral Pueblo people, who lived in the area from 600 to 1300 A.D.. The Cliff Palace, once home to about 100 Native Americans, is an hour's drive from the park entrance. The Cliff Palace Loop Road, open 8:00 a.m. to sunset, takes you past Cliff Palace, Balcony House, and overlooks to other cliff dwellings. Visitors can enter the two popular sites by ranger-guided tour only, so purchase tickets at the Far View Visitor Center before heading out.

A Native American participates in a dance at a pow-wow—an uncommon event, but one of the unique ways that local tribes continue to have a presence in the park.

Step back more than 1,000 years in time when you visit Chaco Culture National Historical Park in New Mexico. Check out the star-studded skies on your own or attend one of the park's night-sky programs, offered several times a week from April through October. The park even has its own observatory.

Chaco Culture's striking landscape is the perfect backdrop for pondering ancestral Puebloan culture as you wander among the impressive remains of their stone buildings.

If you find yourself in Santa Fe, why not take a day trip to Pecos National Historical Park, just 25 miles to the east? You might know that the park is home to the ruins of an Indian pueblo as well as those of a Spanish mission, but did you know you can also visit a stage stop on the Santa Fe Trail, walk the grounds where a Civil War battle unfolded, or fly fish in the Pecos River?

Nicknamed "Queen of the Missions," Mission San José y San Miguel de Aguayo is the area's largest mission. Check out the park's visitor center, sited adjacent to Mission San José; tour the mission church; and don't forget to visit the restored grist mill where wheat was once ground into flour for the mission's inhabitants.

The wooden pews are full on Palm Sunday at Mission San José within San Antonio Missions National Historical Park. The 18th-century missions of this park remain active parishes and have regular services, some of which are conducted in Spanish.

Rock art can be found throughout the national parks of the Southwest. Petroglyphs—such as these animal figures in Arches National Park, Utah—are carvings in the rock's surface. Pictographs, on the other hand, are figures, shapes, and symbols that have been painted on rock surfaces.

If you visit South Dakota's Mount Rushmore National Monument during the summer, consider staying for an evening ranger program or to see the nightly lighting of the presidential visages.

WASHINGTON MONUMENT

The blooming of pink and white cherry blossoms is a sign that spring has arrived in the nation's capital. If you plan your visit for late March or April, you'll be one of the hundreds of thousands of people that get to experience the National Cherry Blossom Festival. **OPPOSITE:** One of most widely recognized landmarks in the nation's capital, the Washington Monument makes for a stunning photography subject at night as well as during the day. You really can't miss it as you stroll among the memorials before hitting the museums that line the National Mall.

1

2

The Battle of Gettysburg was a turning point in the Civil War, the Union victory that ended General Robert E. Lee's second and most ambitious invasion of the North. Gettysburg was the war's bloodiest battle, with 51,000 casualties. It was also the inspiration for President Abraham Lincoln's immortal "Gettysburg Address." Warren Statue, Little Round Top, one of 1,400 monuments and markers within the park that commemorate those who fought in the battle (1). A woman in historic garb (2) lights luminaries in the cemetery on the anniversary of Lincoln's Gettysburg Address, November 19, always a special time to visit the site.

Sunrise silhouette of monument and cannons at Antietam National Battlefield at Sharpsburg, Maryland, where 23,000 soldiers were killed, wounded, or missing in only 12 hours of combat on September 17, 1862. The Battle of Antietam ended the Confederate Army of Northern Virginia's first invasion into the North and led Abraham Lincoln to issue the preliminary Emancipation Proclamation.

OPPOSITE: Hundreds of marchers standing together after crossing the Edmund Pettus Bridge (ABOVE) on the Selma to Montgomery National Historic Trail in Selma, Alabama, in 2010, as part of the Bridge Crossing Jubilee that commemorates the events of "Bloody Sunday." As nonviolent marchers crossed the bridge in 1965, they were tear-gassed, beaten, and had their processional stopped by law-enforcement officers. This unprovoked display of violence was captured by the news media and broadcast worldwide. Two weeks later, another march was held, this time with state and federal law-enforcement protection. Twenty-five thousand marchers concluded the historic journey on March 25 and listened as Dr. Martin Luther King, Jr. and other notable speakers addressed the crowd. As a result of this historic event, the Voting Rights Act was passed on August 6, 1965.

The Statue of Liberty, a gift from the people of France to the people of the United States, was dedicated on October 28, 1886, and designated a national monument in 1924. Buy a ticket on the ferry leaving from Battery Park and you can visit Lady Liberty and Ellis Island (pictured in the background) and learn about the 12 million immigrants who crossed oceans (between January 1892 and November 1954) to become American citizens.

San Juan Island
North Cascades
Ebey's Landing
Ross Lake
Olympic
Lake Chelan
Klondike Gold Rush
Lake Roosevelt
Lewis and Clark
WASHINGTON
Glacier
Mount Rainier
Fort Vancouver
Nez Perce
MONTANA
Fort Union Trading Post
NORTH DAKOTA
Voyageurs
Whitman Mission
Grant-Kohrs Ranch
John Day Fossil Beds
Big Hole
Theodore Roosevelt
Knife River Indian Villages
OREGON
IDAHO
Bighorn Canyon
Little Bighorn Battlefield
MINNESOTA
Crater Lake
Yellowstone
Oregon Caves
John D. Rockefeller, Jr., Parkway
Devils Tower
SOUTH DAKOTA
Mississippi
Redwood
Craters of the Moon
Grand Teton
Mount Rushmore
Lava Beds
Hagerman Fossil Beds
Jewel Cave
Minuteman Missile
Pipestone
Whiskeytown-Shasta-Trinity
Minidoka
WYOMING
Wind Cave
Badlands
Lassen Volcanic
City of Rocks
Niobrara
Missouri
IOWA
Golden Spike
Fossil Butte
Fort Laramie
Agate Fossil Beds
Timpanogos Cave
Scotts Bluff
NEBRASKA
Point Reyes
Dinosaur
NEVADA
Great Basin
Rocky Mountain
Homestead
UTAH
COLORADO
Yosemite
Colorado
Black Canyon
Nicodemus
Harry S Truman
Devils Postpile
Arches
of the Gunnison
Florissant Fossil Beds
Brown v. Board
Pinnacles
Capitol Reef
Canyonlands
Curecanti
Sand Creek Massacre
of Education
Kings Canyon
Cedar Breaks
Natural Bridges
KANSAS
Manzanar
Zion
Bryce
Hovenweep
Bent's Old Fort
Fort Larned
Tallgrass Prairie
Sequoia
Death Valley
Canyon
Glen
Yucca House
Great Sand Dunes
Fort Scott
Pipe Spring
Canyon
Mesa Verde
CALIFORNIA
Lake Mead
Rainbow
Navajo
Bridge
Grand Canyon
Aztec Ruins
Capulin Volcano
George Washington Carver
Channel Islands
Canyon de Chelly
Chaco Culture
Pea Ridge
Mojave
Sunset Crater Volcano
Wupatki
Fort Union
Santa Monica
Hubbell Trading Post
Bandelier
Pecos
Mountains
Tuzigoot
Walnut Canyon
Lake Meredith
Washita Battlefield
Joshua
Montezuma Castle
Petrified
El Morro
Petroglyph
OKLAHOMA
Tree
Forest
El Malpais
Alibates Flint
Fort
ARIZONA
Salinas Pueblo Missions
Quarries
Smith
Cabrillo
Tonto
NEW MEXICO
Hohokam Pima
Casa Grande
Gila Cliff Dwellings
Chickasaw
Ruins
Organ Pipe Cactus
Saguaro
Fort Bowie
White Sands
President William Jefferson
Tumacacori
Chiricahua
Clinton Birthplace Home
Coronado
Chamizal
Carlsbad Caverns
Guadalupe Mountains
TEXAS
Fort Davis
Big Thicket
Lyndon B.
Rio Grande
Johnson
Amistad
San Antonio
Big Bend
Missions

**SAN FRANCISCO
AREA**
Eugene O'Neill
Fort Point
John Muir
Golden Gate
Muir Woods
Port Chicago Naval Magazine
Rosie the Riveter/World War II Home Front
San Francisco Maritime

Cape Krusenstern
Noatak
Gates of the Arctic
Bering Land Bridge
Kobuk Valley
Padre Island
ALASKA
Yukon-Charley Rivers
Palo Alto Battlefield
Denali
Wrangell-St. Elias
Lake Clark
Klondike
HAWAI'I
Gold Rush
Alagnak
Kenai Fjords
Kalaupapa
Katmai
Glacier Bay
World War II
Valor in the Pacific
Haleakalā
Aniakchak
Pu'ukoholā Heiau
Kaloko-Honokōhau
Sitka
Pu'uhonua o Hōnaunau
Hawai'i Volcanoes

MAP OF U.S. NATIONAL PARK UNITS

BOSTON AREA
Adams
Boston African American
Boston Harbor Islands
Boston
Frederick Law Olmsted
John Fitzgerald Kennedy
Longfellow House-Washington's Headquarters
Minute Man
Salem Maritime
Saugus Iron Works

Eleanor Roosevelt
Home of Franklin D. Roosevelt
Vanderbilt Mansion

NEW YORK CITY AREA
African Burial Ground
Castle Clinton
Federal Hall
Gateway (also N.J.)
General Grant
Governors Island
Hamilton Grange
Sagamore Hill
Saint Paul's Church
Statue of Liberty
Theodore Roosevelt Birthplace

WASHINGTON, D.C. AREA
DISTRICT OF COLUMBIA
Carter G. Woodson Home
Constitution Gardens
Ford's Theatre
Franklin Delano Roosevelt Memorial
Frederick Douglass
Korean War Veterans Memorial
Lincoln Memorial
Lyndon Baines Johnson Memorial Grove
Mary McLeod Bethune Council House
National Capital Parks
National Mall
Pennsylvania Avenue
Rock Creek
Theodore Roosevelt Island
Thomas Jefferson Memorial
Vietnam Veterans Memorial
Washington Monument
White House
World War II Memorial

MARYLAND
Antietam
Catoctin Mountain
Chesapeake and Ohio Canal (also D.C., W.Va.)
Clara Barton
Fort Washington
Greenbelt
Monocacy
Piscataway
Potomac Heritage Trail (also Pa., Va., D.C.)
Thomas Stone

VIRGINIA
Arlington House, The Robert E. Lee Memorial
George Washington Birthplace
George Washington Memorial Parkway (also Md.)
Manassas
Prince William Forest
Wolf Trap

UNITED STATES TERRITORIES

AMERICAN SAMOA   **GUAM**   **PUERTO RICO**   **VIRGIN ISLANDS**

National Park of
American Samoa

War in the Pacific

San Juan

Virgin Islands
Virgin Islands Coral Reef
Buck Island Reef
Salt River Bay
Christiansted

Note: Map not to scale

PHOTO CREDITS